Twelve *Ordinary* Men

A BELIEVER'S GUIDE TO
SHARING YOUR FAITH

R C HETRICK

ISBN 979-8-88540-339-9 (paperback)
ISBN 979-8-88540-340-5 (digital)

Christian Faith Publishing
832 Park Avenue
Meadville, PA 16335
www.christianfaithpublishing.com

Printed in the United States of America

INTRODUCTION

Some time ago I was having one of those days. I think it's safe to say we've all had one of those days where we're not feeling too particularly close to God. In my case, I had pushed him away because he was calling me to do something and I didn't want to listen. On this particular day, I was feeling uneasy and kind of uncomfortable. I started thinking about what God was calling me to do. And I felt unprepared, unworthy, and certainly unqualified. After all, I'm just an ordinary guy with a high school diploma and an ordinary job. I was totally giving God what I call the "Moses syndrome." You know, that's where we give God a list of reasons it's not a good idea for us to do what he's asking us to do.

You see, a while back, I was reading my Bible. And I had this thought: *If twelve ordinary men could make the kind of impact on the world that Jesus's disciples made, what kind of impact can twelve ordinary people from every Bible-believing church in America make on the world today?* That's when I felt God's spirit urging me to write a book. Well, I had no background (or desire) to write a book. I had no education on how to write a book. *I had no clue how to write a book or what to write in it!* For the next several months, God began to give me some thoughts that I began to write down. Before I knew it, I had pages of thoughts written down. That's when that "particular day" rolled around. "Journaling thoughts and writing a book are two different things," I said. Or are they? Well, I decided to give up on my will and submit to God's (not without some bumps and hurdles along the way and submitting my will to his daily)—hence the reason for this book.

This book is for the believer first, but it is also for the unbeliever—just ordinary folks who feel that they are unprepared, unworthy, and unqualified to answer God's call as I did. If you are a nonbeliever, God's call on your life is to start a relationship with him through his Son, Jesus Christ. At any time during the reading of this book, if you would like to start that relationship, there is a prayer in the back of the book that you can pray with a sincere heart. And you can start a new life in Christ where you can come to know him intimately, not just know about him.

In this book, we will look at Jesus's disciples and get a better sense of just who they were and why Jesus might have selected them for the task that he would ultimately charge them with. We will also take a look at why, what, where, when, and how Jesus came and taught. It is my hope and prayer that by the end of this book, you will be able to say "I will do that" to my final questions.

I believe we are living in the time that will usher in the rapture of Jesus's church. I'm not trying to be prophetic. This is just an observation. As Christ followers I believe we all should be aware (1 Pet. 4:7) of the things going on in our world today and how they correlate with biblical predictions of the last days. There are too many things in our daily news that line up with these predictions of the end times. Although prophecy and the end times are a topic for a different book (written by someone a lot smarter than me), what I see happening in the world today gives me a feeling of great urgency, as it should every believer, to answer the call on all our lives to spread the gospel: "as you go make disciples" (Matt. 28:19). This action should be a part of our daily lives as it was for Jesus's disciples. Many of us aren't really sure how to make that action a part of our daily lives. Hopefully, this book will assist you in sharing the gospel of Jesus Christ "as you go" with confidence.

THE BOOK

Jesus Christ had many men and women as followers—all of them flawed and imperfect and, yes, all of them sinners. But, despite their flaws, Jesus saw something in them. The first people at Jesus's tomb were women, one of them a former prostitute. Mark, who wrote one of the Gospels, was the center of quite a contentious disagreement between Paul and Barnabas as to whether or not Mark should even join them in the ministry (Acts 15:37–39). He was young, immature, and a deserter. And what about Paul? He said of himself that "he does things that he shouldn't do and doesn't do things that he should" (Rom. 7:15). Can you relate to any of these people? Let's take a look at some of the twelve whom Jesus handpicked to continue his ministry after his ascension. One thing to keep in mind about Jesus's disciples is that the messiah they were looking for was going to end the oppression of Roman rule over them. They might have even been looking for a revolution led by Jesus. What they didn't seem to comprehend until Pentecost was that

Jesus's "revolution" would be against the oppression of sin, not Romans.

There was a song on the radio. I don't know the title or who sings it, but in the song, some lyrics refer to the disciples as a "motley crew of misfits." I like that description of them because that is exactly who they were. They were just ordinary guys with ordinary jobs who after encountering Jesus did extraordinary things for the kingdom of God. As believers, our desire in following Jesus should be that God would use us to do extraordinary things for his kingdom. Whether you're a man or woman reading this book, I believe that you will be able to relate to some of these men and their strengths and weaknesses. Don't make the mistake of assuming that Jesus's disciples were special or even saintly. They were common, ordinary guys with common, ordinary jobs. However, they were men whom we can and should learn from today. Let's take a closer look at some of these men.

Andrew

Andrew, according to John's Gospel, was a follower of John the Baptist. We don't really hear much about Andrew, except that after encountering Jesus he went and told his brother Simon that they had found the Messiah. So Andrew took Simon to meet Jesus (John 1:40–42). I believe Andrew was a man who didn't care about prestige, being out front, or being in the limelight. Walter L. Underwood wrote a book called *Contemporary Twelve*, which I will be referencing throughout this book. He said of Andrew:

> Precedence, place, and honor seem to have meant nothing to Andrew. All that mattered was that he was a follower of Jesus and that he could play his part well, however small it might be.

Also, he said:

> Those who play secondary parts and those who play primary parts should be recognized as of equal importance because it takes the same amount of skill, competence, and commitment to play either role.

I heard once that in an orchestra the second chair may be more important than the first chair because the second chair has to know the first and second chair parts as an understudy would do.

Andrew is the one who brought the boy who had five loaves and two fish to Jesus (John 6:8–9). He performed his role in Jesus's ministry to his full potential and was content with that. What about you? Are you content with the role God has called you to play? I'm sure Andrew struggled with some of the same things that you and I struggle with. But when we have our eyes and focus on Jesus and obediently carry out the task he has called us to with contentment, those struggles that we might encounter along the way are diminished. God gives us grace and strength to overcome our struggles so that we might do extraordinary things for his kingdom. It seems Andrew's calling in life, if you will, was to bring others to Jesus. And he was content with that. At the end of his life, Andrew was to be crucified. At his request, he was crucified on an X-shaped cross. He felt unworthy to hang and die on a cross shaped like his Savior's. Have you answered God's call on your life?

PHILIP

Underwood's description of Philip is "Philip is the least colorful of all the disciples; he was dull, unimaginative, hesitant, vacillating, phlegmatic, apathetic." And I would add *indecisive*. With all that against him, he was still one of the first to be called by Jesus to "follow me" (John 1:43). He was from the same town as Andrew and Simon. He might have also been a fisherman, an ordinary job in that region.

Philip found Nathaniel and told him about Jesus. When next we read about Philip in John, chapter 6, he was basically rebuking Jesus after he was asked, "Where can we buy bread for these people to eat?" He looked at the size of the crowd and told Jesus it was impossible to feed all these people (John 6:7, my paraphrase). Have you ever looked at the size of the mountain you're facing and told Jesus, "That's impossible!"? And how did Philip handle the request he got from the Greeks to "go see Jesus" (John 12:21)? He must have thought Jesus is our Messiah, a Jewish Messiah. What did these

Greeks want of him? His reluctance and indecision about the situation led him to finally tell Andrew, and then they told Jesus. I believe he also overanalyzed the situation, which led to paralyzation, or not taking any action. He could have simply taken the Greeks to Jesus himself. Are you the kind of person who leaps without looking, or do you look so long that you never leap? Before I throw Philip too far under the bus, we can read in the book of Acts that he was appointed as an elder in the early church (Acts 6:5). He evangelized in Samaria and led the Ethiopian eunuch to know Jesus (Acts 8:4–39). He might have also had a powerful ministry in Carthage in North Africa. In Asia Minor, he converted the wife of a Roman proconsul. In retaliation the proconsul had him arrested and brutally put to death.

Nathaniel/ Bartholomew

He is known in the Bible as both Nathaniel and Bartholomew, although some scholars reject the notion that they were the same person. Some scholars agree that Bartholomew might have been his last name.

He was the disciple who when Philip told him about Jesus of Nazareth said, "Can anything good come from Nazareth?" (Man, did he get that wrong!)

To this Philip replied, "Come and see."

And he did. Nathaniel's skepticism may have been a flaw in his character. However, he was quick to confess Jesus was the Son of God (John 1:47–49). Are you a skeptic? Do you underestimate the outcome of a situation or the potential of a person? Nathaniel had widespread missionary travels attributed to him by tradition; he went to India with

Thomas and back to Armenia and also to Ethiopia and Southern Arabia. There are various accounts of how he met his death as a martyr for the gospel.

THOMAS

Who hasn't heard of or used the phrase *doubting Thomas*? Unfortunately for him, this is what most of us think of when someone brings his name up. He seemed to be skeptical about almost everything. In John 14:4–6, Jesus told his disciples that they "knew the way to the place he was going to."

So didn't Thomas say, "Lord [notice he used Jesus's kingly title], we don't know where you are going, so how can we know the way?"

Jesus's response to all the disciples was one of the most famous quotes from him in all the Bible: "I am the way, the truth, and the life. No one comes to the Father except through me."

I believe Thomas's skepticism was one of the traits that led him to follow Jesus in the first place. Why do we only remember him for and focus on his doubt and skepticism? Why don't we remember his commitment to Jesus or his courage? Is it because we can relate to his weakness more than his strengths? I believe that both his commitment and courage come to light in the story of Lazarus's death and resurrection (John 11:16). It may have been a little misplaced; nevertheless, his conviction was there. (Remember Jesus's disciples were looking for a messiah who would end Roman oppression.) What are your convictions, and how far are you willing to go to stand up for them?

There should be no "doubt" that Thomas loved Jesus. To be fair, put yourself in his shoes (or sandals). He had just gone through the whole experience of his friend and Messiah being brutally beaten and put to death. (Even though he might not have witnessed Jesus's crucifixion, I'm sure he was well aware of how crucifixion was carried out.) So now sometime later, the other disciples had told him that they had seen the Lord alive. If you were him, what would your response have been? I want to cut Thomas some slack on the whole doubting thing because I'm not so sure that all of us wouldn't have responded the exact same way. But praise God that Jesus is so full of grace! He gave Thomas exactly what he needed to believe. And what was Thomas's reply? "My Lord and my God" (John 20:24–28). I would give Thomas credit for at least one thing. When he was in, his conviction and compassion drove him to be *all* in. Doubt is nothing to be ashamed of. It is nothing to feel guilty for. In most instances, doubt leads us to question what it is that caused us to doubt. That questioning can lead us to knowledge and understanding, which can lead us to, or bring us back to, faith. If Thomas hadn't doubted the disciples' proclamation that Jesus had risen from the grave, then he would not have been given the opportunity to touch Jesus's hands and side, which brought him to an even stronger and deeper faith.

Tradition has Thomas preaching the gospel of Jesus Christ as far east as India, where the ancient Mar Thoma Christians revere him as their founder. It is said that he died a martyr's death when pierced through with the spears of four soldiers.

Matthew

Tax time! April 15th. For some people, the mere mention of this time of year brings them stress and anxiety. I don't know anyone who enjoys the tax season, except maybe those who receive money back from the IRS. Most people fear getting audited by "the taxman." Although I guess there is some need for taxes, it's hard to like someone who takes some of our hard-earned money just because someone else says that they should do so. That is who Matthew was. He was an educated man to some degree because as a tax collector he would have had to be able to speak more than one language. He was instructed by the ruling power, the Romans, to collect taxes from his countrymen. The tax collectors of Jesus's day were hated by the people for their dishonest practices. They would overcharge the people and keep the overage for themselves. That's called extortion. What kind of person would do that to his own people?

In Mark's Gospel, chapter 2, verses 13–17, we see the phrase *tax collectors and sinners* mentioned four times. This would have been as low as a person could get in the eyes of the people. Why would Jesus call someone like this? Obviously he saw something in Matthew that others didn't. I believe that Jesus would have seen and/or had many encounters with the men he chose before he actually called them to follow him, including Matthew. Think about this. If Joseph, Jesus's earthly father, was dead by this point in Jesus's life—and I believe he was—then Jesus, being the oldest son, would probably have been the one to take care of his mother's affairs, including paying taxes. Even if that wasn't the case, Jesus still would have had to pay his own taxes. And since he was living in that region, I believe that Jesus would have paid his taxes to Matthew for some time before he actually called him to follow.

Whatever kind of person Matthew was when he was called to follow, he didn't hesitate. He immediately left his work behind and followed Jesus. That meant leaving a substantial income. Walter L. Underwood says this about Matthew:

> Apparently, Matthew needed to believe. Can you imagine how it must have been to spend your day extorting and cheating poor people and widows, and literally, taking

bread out of the mouths of children,
for no other reason than to increase
your own bank account? Can you
imagine the guilt, the shame, and
the uselessness he felt leading that
kind of existence, with no purpose
or meaning?

Matthew must have been hoping for or maybe anxiously anticipating Jesus's call on his life. I believe that at some level he knew or at least suspected that Jesus was the Messiah they had all been looking for. Why else would he have immediately left everything to follow Jesus? Whatever the circumstances were that led up to his call, Matthew was ready to follow Jesus. Are you? We can say what we want about the people we don't like. The truth of the matter is that God works best through flaws and weaknesses in character, even our own.

Matthew was one of the earliest writers of the Gospel. He went on to minister in Persia and Ethiopia. There are conflicting reports as to his death pertaining to whether he was martyred or not. At the very least, we know he sacrificed a very lucrative job to follow Jesus. And his life was changed forever. What are you willing to sacrifice to follow Jesus?

JOHN

How would you like to be the one known as "the disciple whom Jesus loved"? Imagine the kind of relationship you would have had with Jesus in order to have the privilege of carrying that title. We know that Jesus loved all his disciples. But John obviously had a more special, maybe deeper, relationship with Jesus as did James, his brother, and Peter. It's no secret that these three were very close to Jesus—his "inner circle," if you will. John was the youngest of all the disciples, maybe still a teenager. He always seemed to be around Jesus. I have this idea that he stayed so close to Jesus that every time Jesus would have to back up or turn around, he would bump into John. Charles R. Brown describes John like this: John, half of the "sons of thunder" duo, was hot-tempered, impetuous, bombastic, exclusive, ambitious, selfish, undisciplined, prejudiced, and intolerant. He was a radical from the word go. On one occasion John and his brother stopped a man from casting out demons and forbade him from doing it again.

Then they rushed to Jesus, probably bursting with self-righteousness, and said, "Master, we saw a man casting out demons in your name, and we forbade him because he does not follow us."

Jesus rebuked them and said, "Do not forbid him, for he that is not against you is for you" (Luke 9:49–50).

On another occasion, it's unclear if it was James and John or their mother who asked Jesus if they could sit at his left hand and at his right hand in Jesus's coming kingdom. Even the other disciples were repelled by such raw and greedy ambition. It seems clear to me at least early in Jesus's ministry these two were, shall we say, a handful.

It is very interesting to me to see how in just three years Jesus's influence on his disciples changed their lives dramatically. He didn't change their character necessarily; he changed their hearts and their perspective. He will do the same for us, too, if we let him. He leaves our character intact because, as I've said before, Jesus uses both our strengths and our weaknesses to accomplish *his* will in and through us to do extraordinary things for his kingdom.

John sat next to Jesus at the Last Supper. He was most likely the only disciple at the cross when Jesus was crucified. In fact, Jesus entrusted the care of his mother, Mary, to John. In that culture, this was the greatest compliment that Jesus could pay him. John is the only disciple who is generally thought to have died a natural death of old age. He was the leader of the church in the Ephesus area and is said to have taken care of Mary in his home. During Domitian's persecution in the middle AD 90s, he was exiled to the island of Patmos where he is credited with writing the last book of the New Testament: the Revelation. An early Latin tradition has him escaping unharmed after being cast into boiling oil in Rome.

PETER

His given name was Simon. He was the brother of Andrew. These two were of the first disciples called to follow Jesus. Peter was full of life, bold, daring, confident, and very capable. He was an "in your face" kind of guy. He would act first and think second. Even though we know him to have denied Jesus three times, he was a very committed person. When he was in, he was all in. As Jesus's disciple, he was fully engaged at all times. Jesus saw enough good qualities in him that in spite of his bad qualities or character flaws, Jesus still decided to use him to build his church (Matt. 16:18). I think Jesus changed his name from Simon to Peter (which means "rock") because he knew Peter's character was solid and that he would be up to the challenge.

Did Peter deny Jesus not once but three times? Yes. Did he draw his sword in the garden and cut off the ear of the servant of the high priest? Some say so. Was he too impetuous and maybe a little arrogant? Probably. Did he lose faith sometimes? Don't we all? Remember, though, Peter was the only one to get out of the boat and walk on water even for just a minute before he grew fearful and sank. The great thing is that Jesus saw through all his faults and character flaws, through the rough exterior to the heart and soul of Peter. That's where Jesus found the man who would pioneer the Christian church. Even if you don't think that you have it in you, Jesus can find in each of us someone who will take his gospel to our world if we would commit ourselves to him as Peter did.

Peter was martyred in Rome about AD 66, during the persecution under Emperor Nero. He was crucified upside down at his own request. He did not feel worthy to die in the same manner as his Lord and Savior.

Let me sum up for you who these men were during the three years that they walked with Jesus. At times they were *impulsive, forgetful, thickheaded, outspoken, cowardly, easily distracted, fearful, desperate, stubborn, selfish, preoccupied, arrogant,* and *prideful.* Does any of that describe anyone you know? There is so much more, good and bad, that could be said about these men and the five not mentioned in this book. The most important thing, though, is not who these men were before and even during their encounter with Christ; it's who they were after they spent time with him and ultimately then being filled with his spirit to continue the work Jesus started. That's when they really began to shine for Christ. But take note: at least eight of the twelve died a martyr's death for their faith. That's what I would call "all in." It is very apparent that people are truly changed when they have an encounter with Jesus Christ and go all in to follow him. Are you ready and willing to go all in for Jesus? He went all in for you.

I trust that for the purpose of this book you have grasped the thought I am trying to convey—that twelve ordinary men with flawed character could in fact do extraordinary things for the kingdom of God to impact the whole world through the simple task of sharing the gospel of Jesus Christ. Maybe you don't think that sharing the gospel with your friends, family, neighbors, and/or coworkers is a simple task. I know that some people get very nervous and anxious when it comes to sharing their faith with others. I hope to take the rest of this book and give you some insights that might be helpful in making the gospel of Jesus Christ easier for you to share with people.

Before I do that, though, I would like to mention another group of ordinary men that accomplished something extraordinary together. Today we still have the freedom in the United States to share that gospel, worship together, and express our faith with others. In many countries around the world, people don't have that freedom. And in recent years and months, in these United States, all our freedoms have been under attack. Our forefathers fled to this country to escape religious persecution and build a life for themselves and others that made it possible to live and work free from government oppression. They fought and bled and died for the freedoms they believed in. These men drafted a document that until recent years was held with very high regard to say the least. That is our Constitution and the amendments that followed. Included in these documents is the right or freedom to worship God openly and freely without government interference (the very first amendment). That is changing in this country very rapidly. If you are a believer in Jesus Christ, I pray that God would show you the urgency of the great commission in the times that we are now living because *we don't have much time left, y'all!* I'm not claiming to know the future, but I know the One who does. There is coming a day in the very near future when the church will face persecution like it has never seen. And then the rapture! But remember, though, what Paul said in 2 Timothy 3:12: "Everyone who wants to live a godly life in Christ Jesus will be persecuted, while evil men and impostors will go from bad to worse, deceiving and being deceived." Please don't let this truth make you fearful. God said that he would never leave us nor forsake us. He calls us to persevere in the face of persecution because we know our reward: "Blessed are those who are persecuted because of righteousness, for theirs is the kingdom of heaven" (Matt. 5:10). Are you willing to face persecution for the sake of the gospel? Are you willing to face persecution for the sake of our Constitution of the United States? I pray that you would find a place to start. I strongly recommend that you start with prayer. If you ask Jesus to show up, he will. Face whatever fear you may have and access the power of Jesus Christ that we possess through the Holy Spirit and share your faith with someone. You may find it's easier than you think. Sharing Christ with someone is always worth the effort.

Question: Why did Jesus's disciples leave everything including family to follow him? I believe they knew or could sense that there was something very different about Jesus. What was it about him? Jesus wasn't the ordinary run-of-the-mill revolutionary. He wasn't a zealot. He was from Nazareth for crying out loud! He was trained as a carpenter, not as a flamboyant military strategist. The people were looking for someone with zeal and charisma to save them from Roman rule and oppression. Do you recall in 1 Samuel 9:2 the description of Israel's first king, Saul: "he was an impressive young man without equal among the Israelites—a head taller than any of the others." It says the same thing in 10:23. In 10:24 it says, "There is no one like him among all the people." In 16:7 it says, speaking of

David, "Man looks at the outward appearance but God looks at the heart." Basically the people chose their first king by his looks and stature. Jesus didn't have any of that going for him. In fact, the Bible says in Isaiah 53:2, "He had no beauty or majesty to attract us to him, nothing in his appearance that we should desire him." There was, however, one thing that stood out about Jesus. His miracles notwithstanding, it was his message and the way he delivered it. I believe his teaching was the attraction for the disciples and many others. In Matthew 7:28–29 it says, "The crowds were amazed at his teaching, because he taught as one who had authority, and not as their teachers of the law." Let's look at why Jesus came and what, where, when, and how Jesus taught. This will by no means be an exhaustive list. These are just some of the things that I have found in Scripture that I am using in this book. However, it is the same why, what, where, when, and how we should be using to share the gospel with others today. I would encourage you, though, to do your own study. I'm sure that you will find more examples that may be helpful to you.

1. *Why did Jesus come?* Reconciliation. In Matthew 20:28 Jesus said, "The Son of Man did not come to be served, but to serve, and

to give his life as a ransom for many." He came to obediently shed his blood and die on a cross as the Sacrificial Lamb for the sins of all mankind. And through his sacrifice, he reconciled mankind back to God.

For if, when we were God's enemies, we were reconciled to him through the death of his Son, how much more, having been reconciled, shall we be saved through his life. (Rom. 5:10)

Therefore, if anyone is in Christ, he is a new creation; the old has gone, the new has come! All this is from God, who reconciled us to himself through Christ and gave us the ministry of reconciliation: that God was reconciling the world to himself in Christ, not counting men's sins against them. And he has committed to us the message of reconciliation. We are therefore Christ's ambassadors, as though God were making his appeal through us. We implore you on Christ's behalf: Be reconciled to God. God made him who had no

sin to be sin for us, so that in him
we might become the righteousness
of God. (2 Cor. 5:17–21)

Our sin has created a void or separation
between us and God. The only way to bring
us back into fellowship with or reconcile us
to God is through the shed blood of Jesus
Christ. He was and is and always will be the
only begotten Son of God who lived, as a
man, a perfect sinless life, which qualified
him to be the sacrifice that mankind needed
for reconciliation. You just read that we have
been given the ministry of reconciliation by
God. When we share the gospel with others,
we are executing that ministry. Remember
the commission for this ministry is Matthew
28:19–20: "Go and make disciples of all
nations, baptizing them in the name of the
Father and of the Son and of the Holy Spirit
and teaching them to obey everything I have
commanded you. And surely I am with you
always, to the very end of the age." Where
we are to do this is found in Acts 1:8: "You
will receive power when the Holy Spirit
comes on you; and you will be my witnesses
in Jerusalem, and in all Judea and Samaria,

and to the ends of the earth." I will touch on this a little later. Have you been faithful to this ministry that has been given to us by God? Although we cannot forgive sin ourselves for reconciliation, we can bring people to the One who can.

2. *What did Jesus teach?* Repentance, forgiveness, salvation, relationship. This also is what we should be telling others. People need to repent to receive forgiveness; they need forgiveness to receive salvation; they need salvation to be in a relationship with God, and we all need to be in a relationship with God to accomplish his will while we're on earth. Are you aware that this earth is not our home (1 Pet. 2:11–12)?

a) Jesus is the One who calls us to *repentance.*

The Lord is not slow in keeping his promise, as some understand slowness. He is patient with you, not wanting anyone to perish, but everyone to come to repentance. (2 Pet. 3:9)

[Jesus speaking] I have not come to call the righteous, but sinners to repentance. (Luke 5:32)

When some people are told about repentance, they immediately understand. They are humbled and take action. Other people find repentance to be a hurdle that's hard for them to get over. You may have to work with them to get them over this hurdle. Sometimes these people are struggling to forgive themselves for something they have done or something that they think is unforgivable. This can make it difficult for them to receive forgiveness from a holy God. It may take more effort on your part to help these people understand repentance. Remember God is the One who calls to repentance. We are to help them hear that call.

And how will they hear if no one tells them? (Rom. 10:14)

Why do people need to repent? For the forgiveness of their sins.

b) Jesus is the only One who is able to *forgive* sin.

When Jesus saw their faith, he said to the paralytic, "Son, your sins are forgiven." Now some teachers of the law were sitting there, thinking to themselves, *Why does this fellow talk like that? He's blaspheming! Who can forgive sins but God alone?* Immediately Jesus knew in his spirit that this is what they were thinking in their hearts, and he said to them, "Why are you thinking these things? Which is easier: to say to the paralytic, 'Your sins are forgiven' or to say 'Get up, take your mat and walk.' But that you may know that the Son of Man has authority on earth to forgive sins…" He said to the paralytic, "I tell you, get up, take your mat and go home." He got up, took his mat and walked out in full view of all of them. This amazed everyone and they praised God, saying, "We have never seen anything like this." (Mark 2:5–12)

They said themselves, "Who can forgive sins but God alone?" What the teachers of the law failed to either believe or realize was that the One they were talking about was God in the flesh—Jesus Christ. Isaiah 8:14 says, "He will be a stone that causes men to stumble and a rock that makes them fall." While on earth, Jesus was God in human form. We need to realize that this fact still makes people stumble and fall today. It may take time to help people over this stone. Once people grasp the reality that they are in need of forgiveness and that Jesus is the only One who can meet that need, then they're ready to receive the salvation that's only found in Christ.

c) Jesus is our *salvation*.

[Peter speaking] Salvation is found in no one else, for there is no other name under heaven given to men by which we must be saved. (Acts 4:12)

My soul finds rest in God alone; my salvation comes from him. He

alone is my rock and my salvation.
(Ps. 62:1–2)

Our salvation comes through the shed
blood of Jesus Christ on the cross of Calvary.

The Lord will lay bare his holy
arm in the sight of all nations, and
all the ends of the earth will see the
salvation of our God. (Isa. 52:10)

Many people try to find salvation in
many different things these days.

But you, O God, are my king
from of old; you bring salvation
upon the earth. (Ps. 74:12)

God is the only One who has eternal
salvation that he offers freely. He doesn't
hide his salvation from us. We don't have to
embark on some long pilgrimage to achieve
it. Jesus has already worked out God's plan
of salvation for us.

Sing to the Lord a new song,
for he has done marvelous things;

his right hand and his holy arm
have worked salvation for him. The
Lord has made his salvation known
and revealed his righteousness to the
nations. (Ps. 98:1–2)

All we have to do is believe and receive
it. The salvation that unbelievers look for
is temporary and usually costs them something. That road is also usually paved with
heartache and sorrow. It's our responsibil-
ity to help them see the road they're on and
help them find the road to God's eternal salvation. This salvation can then be received
by God's grace through faith. Who do you
know is on a "road that leads to destruc-
tion" (Matt. 7:13)? Once a person believes
the gospel and receives salvation from God
through Jesus Christ, then they can begin a
new relationship with him.

d) *Relationship*. This is the part that an
   individual will work on their whole life.
   Let's face it. Relationships are hard! At
   least some are. Our relationship with
   Jesus Christ should be the one we work
   the hardest for, the one we give the most

time to. Oftentimes it is the one that is neglected the most. This, I think, is one reason unbelievers have a hard time finding Christ. Most people are looking at professing believers (I don't use the title "Christian" too much. It has become too inclusive and watered down. In many churches Christianity is a club that you join) to find Jesus. If we don't keep our relationship with Jesus nurtured and strong, then he won't be attractive to us. Our relationship with others is only going to be as strong as our relationship with Jesus Christ. Y'all, Jesus is the grace that one sinner needs to love and forgive another sinner.

If your relationship with Jesus is lacking today, you can start making it stronger through prayer and his Word. Study his Word. That is how you spend time with God. How did you get to know your spouse? You spent time with them. You studied them. You got to know their mannerisms, their strengths and flaws, their quirks, their sense of humor (or lack thereof), and their likes and dislikes. That is how you can nurture any relationship. Make the time to spend time with people. But, you say, I don't like people. I have heard people say that the church would be a great place if it weren't for the people. I'll say it again. Jesus is the grace that one sinner needs to love and forgive another sinner. Make time for Jesus in your life.

3. *Where and when did Jesus teach?* These two pretty much go hand in hand. A better translation of Matthew 28:19 is "Going, then, disciple all nations, baptizing them in the name of the Father and of the Son and of the Holy Spirit." It could also be translated as "As you go, disciple all nations." Jesus taught as he went (where). As he journeyed from place to place, he used each moment as a teaching opportunity. He taught at the moment (when).

4. *How did Jesus teach?* If it doesn't already exist, someone could write a book just on this topic. I am just going to highlight a few things:

a) *Jesus taught with authority.* Scripture says that people marveled at his teaching "as one who had authority." Jesus himself said in Matthew 28:18, "All authority in heaven and on earth was given to me." Jesus is the authority in God's Word because he is God's Word. If you are a follower of Jesus Christ, you can speak with the same authority through the power of the Holy Spirit. Are you utilizing this power?

b) *Jesus taught with and by the power of the Holy Spirit.* In Luke 4:16–19, I will paraphrase: Jesus went to Nazareth and on the Sabbath went to the synagogue "as was his custom." He opened the scriptures and read, "The spirit of the Lord is on me because he has anointed me to preach good news to the poor" (18a). All Jesus did was read from the scriptures. But he knew that particular scripture, from Isaiah 61, was prophesying about him. He was using this particular scripture to try to let the people know just who he was, at the same time letting them know how he could teach with authority. That is by God's Holy Spirit. He also knew who he was, which allowed him to teach with confidence. We can speak with this same confidence if we know whose we are.

Also, John 3:34 says, "For the one whom God has sent speaks the words of God, for God gives the Spirit without limit." As believers are we not sent? Do we not have God's Word to speak? Who gives the spirit without limit? God does! I understand that sometimes our tongues get wrapped around our eyeteeth when we try to share our faith with someone. We think that what we said was just a bunch of gravel we chewed up and spit out. One of the great things about our God is that he can use that chewed-up gravel to bring glory and others to himself. But he can't do that if we don't spit out the gravel. And he gives us his spirit to help us do that.

c) *Jesus taught from the scriptures.* You have just read one example of Jesus reading from the scriptures. There are many times when he either read from or quoted scripture. There is nothing that can cut to a person's heart faster and more accurately than God's Word.

The word of God is living and active. Sharper than any double-edged sword, it penetrates even to dividing soul and spirit, joints and marrow; it judges the thoughts and attitudes of the heart. Nothing in all creation is hidden from God's sight. Everything is uncovered and laid bare before the eyes of him to whom we must give an account. (Heb. 4:12–13)

When is the last time you shared God's Word with someone?

d) *Jesus taught with repetition.* You may have heard it said that people are creatures of habit. This is nothing more than a tendency to repeat an action in the same way, to familiarize, and to frequent (Webster's). The family, friends, and coworkers whom you are trying to reach for Christ will need to be reminded often of who Jesus is, how he loves them, what he's done in your life, etc. Repetition. Jesus hasn't called us to a once-and-done ministry. We shouldn't share our faith once with someone and say, "Boy, I'm glad that's over with. That was hard. I hope I don't have to do that again." On the contrary. When we decide to witness to someone, going in we should be devoted to witnessing to and praying for that person for as long as it takes to bring them to Christ. Prayer will do more to help someone find Christ than any words we could ever say (more on this later). We may have occasions where we meet someone one time on a plane or on a vacation or business trip and we never see them again. On those occasions, we still should share Christ with them and then continue to pray for them that the Holy Spirit will do his work in their heart. So we're still not once-and-done. Acts 2:42 is a verse that tells us how the early Christians lived. But I believe it's also a template for how we can witness: "They devoted themselves to the apostles' teaching [devote yourself to reading God's Word] and to the fellowship, to the breaking of bread [be devoted to spending time with them] and to prayer [be devoted to praying for them]." This should be the least that we are willing to do for them. After all, aren't they worth it?

e) *Jesus taught through the culture with relevance.* Matthew 9:14–17 is an example of how Jesus did this. He used the bridegroom, the patch sewn on clothing, and the wineskins to get his point across. These three things were all things that his audience would have been very familiar with in their day-to-day living. As you witness, try to find ways to use the culture and current events to help your audience understand the point you're trying to make. For example, I've used the current virus pandemic to share with people why I'm not afraid of it and that we don't have to live in fear of it or of anything or anyone else. The more you practice, the better you'll get.

f) *Jesus taught through relationships.* Jesus led by example in these relationships. He let his actions speak for him. By doing so he earned the right to be heard by the people with whom he was in a relationship. We need to do the same. I know what you're going to say: "But Jesus was perfect! He was God in the flesh!" He was.

But while he was here, he was "tempted in every way" (Heb. 4:15). But he was empowered by the same Holy Spirit who lives in us if we are a believer. I know that relationships can be difficult, to say the least. Everyone has their own set of circumstances. Throughout my life, none of the relationships that I've had were perfect. Growing up my brother and I fought all the time. At times, throughout my career, I didn't treat all my coworkers the way I should have. On many occasions, I disappointed and let down my wife and boys. But I didn't let these poor decisions on my part defeat me. How we treat people is a choice. We make a conscious and sometimes emotional decision on how we are going to treat someone. How we treat people may be our strongest witness. Jesus always chose to love. This is his greatest example of how we can have great relationships with others. Did you choose to love someone today?

g) *Jesus taught with humility and sincerity.* Jesus wasn't teaching things he himself didn't know and believe. What kind of a witness would we be if we didn't know the

God we were telling others about? If you want to help others find Christ, then you have to have a personal relationship with Christ. That is what sets the Christian faith apart from all other faiths. We can know our God personally because he is alive. For the most part, I feel that it will come naturally to be sincere in our witness if we know God and believe that his Word is true. There may be some people who will make it difficult to be sincere. That's why it's important to be humble as well when we talk to people.

Think about Jesus's encounters with the Pharisees. They were always trying to trap him or catch him saying something contrary to the law. Yet he treated them with the respect that their office required. Jesus knew that if he attacked them, he would lose the attention and respect of the people whom he was trying to save. When Jesus answered the Pharisees' questions, he left them with their dignity. Although his answers may have been embarrassing for the Pharisees, his answers weren't demeaning or untruthful. Jesus didn't put people down for their unbelief. Even when he called them hypocrites, he pointed out why they were being hypocritical. He was humble in his approach to interacting with people. When I was a young Christian, I was attending a church that had an "evangelism" ministry. I joined the ministry that would go door to door telling people about Christ. As a young Christian, I wanted to learn from, shall we say, more "seasoned" or "veteran" Christians. After a few visits, I realized that these veteran Christians were really just beating people up with their Bibles. I questioned these tactics and got the same treatment.

Remember this: when you walk away from a conversation with someone about God, you want them to feel better about themselves and their situation, not worse. Remember this too: it's the Holy Spirit's job to bring conviction to someone's heart, not ours. It is very important that we make sure our communication to others about God is this: *God hates sin but loves sinners!* If God hated sinners, he wouldn't have saved Noah and his family. You can be successful in being both humble and sincere if you keep this in mind whenever you talk to someone about God. After all, we're all sinners, believers and nonbelievers alike.

h) *Jesus taught with stories.* This one doesn't take much to explain. It goes back to being relevant and current to the time we are living in. Jesus used things to tell stories, or parables, that were common to everyone. If you find it difficult coming up with a story like that, then you can use one from the Bible. It doesn't matter if they believe the Bible to be true. God says his Word will not return void. He can use his Word in anyone's heart if we will share it with them.

Also, share your story. God has given you a story to share, not to bury on a shelf. Your story is your life—your hardships, your successes, your struggles, your accomplishments, etc. No one can deny you your story. I know someone who was facing jail time for drug possession. He went on to have a successful evangelistic ministry and is currently pastoring a church. Don't be afraid to tell your story. Do you give God the glory for your story? Be sure that you do.

i) *Jesus taught with love.* This arguably could be the most important one of them all. If we aren't loving, people just won't want to listen. I know what you're going to say. It's hard to love unlovable people. Nobody knows this better than Jesus Christ. When was the last time you hung on a cross and died for someone? Maybe some of you have gone through what seemed like a crucifixion. Some people have given their lives for Christ. I'm sure that some of you reading this have sacrificed much for the cause of Christ. Whatever you sacrificed, you did so because you love God and you love people. That's the bottom line—to love people, even the unlovable. God says in Luke 6:27–28, "Love your enemies, do good to those who hate you, bless those who curse you, and pray for those who mistreat you." That's a tall order maybe even impossible to do in our own strength. That is why God has given us his Holy Spirit. Philippians 4:13 says, "I can do all things through Christ who strengthens me"—even loving unlovable people.

I read someone's commentary on Jesus that said, "Jesus taught and modeled a powerful leadership philosophy that, in his day, was a novel—and confusing—approach." How did Jesus lead, and why was it so confusing for people? *Jesus led by serving others. We need to lead by serving others too!* I can't emphasize enough the importance of serving others—and the windows of opportunity that it will lead to. I'll give you an example.

I am fortunate to have had the opportunity to do ministry at a few different places throughout the States and even the world. On one such occasion, I was on a trip with a group of high school students to Peru. On the flight down, we found out that a certain young lady in our group disliked feet—anything to do with other people's feet. You can imagine in a group of teens how she would have to endure a little harassment for this "feet problem" that she had. Several days into our trip, we were out for a walk through the village we were visiting, and we encountered one of the local boys not far from the compound that we were staying in. He was probably ten or twelve years old and standing on the street corner with a suitcase of goods that he was trying to sell to passersby. In this area, most people walked to wherever they needed to go.

As we approached him to find out what his goods were, this certain young lady noticed that his feet were filthy and cut and bleeding. Soccer is a very popular sport in South American culture. The village we were in was very poor, and many children could not afford shoes to wear, so they would play soccer all day long barefoot. No doubt this boy's feet were a result of this. So this certain young lady ran back to our compound and got a basin of warm soapy water, a towel, bandages, socks, and shoes. She came back and without hesitation began to wash his feet. As his feet began to come clean, we noticed that he was missing a toenail. She was so gentle and caring with him. When she was finished washing his feet, she bandaged them and put brand-new never-worn white socks on him and brand-new never-worn shoes on him—not just any shoes though. She had grabbed a pair of soccer cleats for him. I believe they were Nike cleats. The cleats were probably one size too big for him, but he was elated. To him those cleats were gold. He could not stop thanking her.

Here was a situation where someone saw a need and without hesitating began to serve. As a result of her service, she then had an opportunity to share the gospel with him. That's what it's about, y'all! Serving others with the love of Christ. If you claim to be a Christ follower or believer in Christ, then you, too, have his love in you. How are you sharing that love? To whom are you sharing that love? We serve Jesus Christ by serving others. Will you serve Jesus by serving others even if it requires sacrifice? Will you trust God to work in and through you to impact your world? Remember everything that Jesus did brought glory to God and revealed him to his audience. With the events happening in our world today, people are fearful, if not terrified. Y'all, people need Jesus, and most don't even know it. They have no hope of a future. God lovingly tells us in Jeremiah 29:11, "For I know the plans I have for you, plans to prosper you and not harm you, plans to give you hope and a future." Do you feel that you are prospering today? Do you feel there are those trying to harm you? There are people who do feel this way. That is why the suicide rate has skyrocketed recently. People need the Lord. And I am one who believes that we don't have much time left to share him with them. Let me be very candid. Sharing our faith with others will never be easier than it is right now. It is only going to get more difficult as our world races toward the antichrist agenda that is sprouting up all over the world today. Our sacrifice will become greater and greater in the days ahead. I believe that the church will experience some degree of persecution before the rapture. Don't let this discourage you though. You have God's Holy Spirit within you, giving you his supernatural power to help you endure and overcome anything that comes your way. *Anything!* So take heart for we shall soon see Jesus in all his glory.

Let me ask you something. Who do you know in your life right now is not saved and going to heaven when they die? What is their eternal soul worth to you? What would you be willing to sacrifice to help them find the salvation in Christ that you have? Whom would you like to go to heaven with you when the rapture takes place? Are you sure they're ready? If you like, you can use the prayer that follows to help you help them find Jesus. If you have never started a relationship with Jesus Christ and would like to do that now, I would like to help you do that. If you have read this whole book, you may remember that I talked about four things: repentance, forgiveness, salvation, and relationship. Repentance is first. First, you must agree with God that you are a sinner. Romans 3:23 says, "For all have sinned and fall short of the glory of God." We have all missed the mark of the standard of a sinless life set forth by Jesus Christ. He is the only Man—

God in the flesh—who ever lived a perfect sinless life. He set the standard. We all fall short of that standard. Romans 6:23 says, "The wages of sin is death, but the gift of God is eternal life in Christ Jesus our Lord." The penalty for our sin is death. This is eternal separation from God in hell. That is what the Bible calls the second death. So you must turn from your sinful life and commit yourself to following Jesus. That is what repentance means. You make a complete 180-degree turn from one direction to the opposite direction with his help.

Forgiveness is next. If you agree with God that you are a sinner, then confess your sin to him and ask him to forgive you for your sin. Romans 5:8 says, "God demonstrates his own love for us in this: While we were still sinners, Christ died for us." We owe a debt for our sin that we cannot pay. Christ paid a debt for our sin that he didn't owe. Jesus Christ endured the brutal punishment of crucifixion for the sins of all mankind. You may or may not have heard that before Christ, God required the blood of animals to cover sin. Jesus bled and died once and for all. Salvation! Jesus Christ died on the cross and on the third day was raised from the grave to live again forever. Romans 10:9–10 says, "If you confess with your mouth, 'Jesus is Lord,' and believe in your heart that God raised him from the dead, you will be saved. For it is with your heart that you believe and are justified, and it is with your mouth that you confess and are saved." Salvation comes when you believe and receive the truth of Jesus Christ with your heart. Romans 10:13 says, "Everyone who calls on the name of the Lord will be saved."

Are you ready to call on him? If you are, you can pray a prayer similar to this: "Lord Jesus, I admit that I am a sinner. I understand that my sin has separated me from you, and I don't want to live separated from you anymore. I confess my sin to you now and ask for your forgiveness. I believe that you died on the cross for my sin and on the third day you were raised to life again. Thank you for loving me and paying the price for my sin. Thank you for forgiving me. Help me to follow you with my life from this day forward. Amen."

There is no magic to these words. It's not the words that save you. Talk to him from your heart. If you communicate this to God with a sincere heart, he will save you. 1 Kings 8:39 says, "Forgive and act; deal with each man according to all he does, since you know his heart (for you alone know the hearts of all men)."

Relationship. If you prayed to receive Christ and the salvation he offers, then you are now in a relationship with him. Praise the Lord! Luke 15:7 says, "I tell you that in the same way there will be more rejoicing in heaven over one sinner who repents than over ninety-nine righteous persons who do not need to repent." How do you maintain a relationship with the God of the angel armies? It's actually quite simple when you boil it down. You spend time with him. How do you spend time with the God of the universe? You read and pray and pray and read. Read God's Word daily. The Bible is God's written Word to us. Also, try to live a life of prayer. Give him thanks continually. Praise him always. Lift others up to him in accessory prayer.

Earlier I spoke of the founding fathers of the United States of America and the freedoms they fought and died for. The only real freedom anyone has is in their relationship with their Creator—the Creator of the universe, the Son of God, the Prince of peace, our eternal salvation, Jesus Christ. If you surrender your life to him today, you will never be the same. You, too, will be ready to do extraordinary things for his kingdom.

About the Author

Ron has been married to his sweetheart for forty-three years. Together they have two grown children. He has worked in residential construction his whole career including many years as a cabinet maker. He has helped to plant several churches and volunteered in many ministry roles throughout the years. Ron is a former Associate Pastor at Outbreak Church in Rock Hill, SC. His passion is for authentic believers in Jesus Christ to understand how important it is to boldly share the truth of God's word with others and to realize their role in spreading the Gospel. Especially in today's world, the church can't sit on the sideline while lost souls are perishing all around us. He believes there is not much time left to reach lost people with the good news of Jesus Christ.